DATE DUE

MAR 1 5 '02			
OCT 1 0 2006			
NOV 1 6 2006			
OCT 0 5 2011			

Demco, Inc. 38-293

Everything You Need to Know About

DRUG ABUSE

Many teens consider drinking alcohol and smoking cigarettes a rite of passage.

Everything You Need to Know About

DRUG ABUSE

Dr. Arthur G. Herscovitch

THE ROSEN PUBLISHING GROUP, INC.
NEW YORK

Published in 1998 by The Rosen Publishing Group, Inc.
29 East 21st Street, New York, NY 10010

Library of Congress Cataloging-in-Publication Data

Herscovitch, Arthur, 1947—
    Everything you need to know about drug abuse / Arthur G. Herscovitch—1st ed.
    p.   cm.—(The need to know library)
    Includes bibliographical references and index.
    Summary: Provides information on drugs and their harmful effects, as well as how to avoid drugs and where to get help for drug abuse problems.
        ISBN 0-8239-2624-9
        1. Drug abuse—United States—Juvenile literature. 2. Drug abuse—United States—Prevention—Juvenile literature. 3. Teenagers—Drug abuse—United States—Juvenile literature. [1. Drug abuse.] I. Title. II. Series.
    HV5809.5.H49 1998
    362.29′0973—dc21   97-49430
                                                                                    CIP
                                                                                    AC

Manufactured in the United States of America

Contents

Introduction

*J*anice was in a lousy mood as she sat in the principal's office. She was waiting for her mother to come to school. Janice had been caught smoking marijuana on school grounds and was about to be expelled.

This was not the first time that Janice had got in trouble. But things had not always been this way with Janice. At one time she didn't mind going to school. Her grades were pretty good, too. But Janice is quiet and shy, and she never had many friends. Then one day after school, Janice was offered some pot by two popular girls. Janice wasn't sure if she really wanted to try the marijuana. On the other hand, she really wanted the girls to like her.

At first Janice didn't like the bitter taste of the smoke. It made her cough. Marijuana also made her feel light-headed and dizzy. But it was important to her to be accepted. Over the next few weeks she smoked more and *more with her new friends. She got used to how it made her feel—and she started to like it. She laughed a lot when she was high. She felt more outgoing, and she started going to parties. But as Janice found herself smoking more pot, she began to lose interest in school. She didn't pay attention in class and she stopped doing her homework. Her grades went down, and sometimes she came to class stoned.*

Now, Janice is on the verge of being kicked out of school. Even though she is playing it cool, deep down, she doesn't want to be expelled. She feels really bad about what's happening to her life.

Drug abuse is a growing problem in the United States among teenagers. According to the National Institute on Drug Abuse, the use of illegal drugs by adolescents increased significantly between 1992 and 1995. In addition, many teens underestimate the risks of drug abuse, and they have greater access to illegal drugs than ever before. This book talks about drug abuse and the various types of drugs that can be abused.

Maybe you are curious about drugs. Maybe, like Janice, you're feeling pressure to take them. Or maybe you're using drugs now. Whatever the case, this book gives you information about drugs and their harmful effects. It also talks about how to avoid using drugs, or if you are using them, how to stop. Hopefully, you'll find the information you need to help you stay away from drugs and find better things to do with your life.

All drugs can have negative effects on the body.

Chapter 1

What Are Drugs?

A drug is any chemical you take that changes how you think, feel, or act. Some drugs are legal, and they may be bought over-the-counter at drugstores. Some drugs are used to treat illnesses but are legal only when they are prescribed by a doctor. Other drugs are legal but have certain limitations, such as alcohol, which can be used only by people over twenty-one, and tobacco, which can only be bought by people over eighteen. Caffeine is a drug found in many familiar products, such as coffee, tea, soda, and chocolate. There are no restrictions on caffeine—it can be used by people of any age.

All drugs can be harmful: legal drugs that are taken for too long or in too large a dosage; medicines used illegally without a prescription; illegal drugs used to get high. But legal or not, any drug can be abused, and possibly lead to drug dependency, also called addiction. Drug abuse can produce many physical and psychological problems. This chapter discusses the many different types of drugs and the short- and long-term effects they have on your body.

Alcohol

Alcohol is a depressant. At first it may make a person feel high, but it lowers the heart rate and slows down the central nervous system. The alcohol is absorbed directly into the bloodstream; it affects a person's coordination, dulls the senses, and can cause memory loss.

Despite the fact that it's illegal for anyone under twenty-one to drink alcohol, many teens have easy access to it. For most teens it is the first drug they try. Many are unaware of the harmful effects of alcohol. Binge drinking (consuming large amounts of alcohol in a short time) is especially dangerous. It can cause alcohol poisoning and put a person in a coma. It is a growing problem among teens and college students.

Caffeine

Caffeine is probably the most widely used drug in the world. Most of us associate caffeine with coffee. Between 82 and 92 percent of Americans drink coffee. Caffeine is a stimulant. It makes users feel more alert, increasing the heart rate and blood pressure. In large doses, caffeine can make a person anxious and nervous and cause stomach problems. In addition to coffee, tea, and soda, caffeine can be found in common medicines and "stay awake" drugs like NoDoz and Vivarin.

Depressants

Depressants are among the most popular drugs in the United States. They are prescribed to treat people who suffer from anxiety, insomnia (sleeplessness), and stress. Many people are helped by depressants, such as Valium and Xanax, when they are used correctly. Under a doctor's care and supervision, they can be safe.

But many people abuse them. Depressants produce a feeling similar to alcohol. Users feel euphoric in the beginning, but then they get sleepy and slur their speech. Depressants can pose great risks to both legal and illegal users. Abusing them can lead to addiction, which can be life-threatening.

Hallucinogens

These drugs include LSD (acid), PCP (angel dust), mush-rooms, and mescaline. When someone takes a hallu-cinogen, the sense of time and place becomes distorted. In other words, a user sees, hears, and feels things that aren't really there. Hallucinogens increase heart rate and blood pressure. They reduce muscle coordination and pain awareness and cause insomnia. They are some of the most common drugs abused by teens. People high on hallucinogens put themselves and others at risk. Users may put their lives in danger by taking unrea-sonable risks or acting violently toward others. The

Depressants can be used safely to help treat anxiety and insomnia. Abusing them, however, can be life-threatening.

effects of hallucinogens are very unpredictable and can last for twelve hours. A user can never be certain how he or she will act while "tripping."

Inhalants

Inhalants are substances that are sniffed. They include airplane glue, nail polish remover, gasoline, solvents, plastic cement, and lighter fluid. Inhalants are found in many cleaning products. These chemicals are easy to buy and use, but even one-time use can be fatal. Inhalants increase heart rate, making a user feel dizzy and light-headed. Inhalants are dangerous because they can cause asphyxia, which stops the flow of oxygen to the brain. This can cause a user to become unconscious.

Other risks include cardiac arrest (heart attack) and suffocation. Over time, a user risks damaging the brain, lungs, liver, and kidneys.

Marijuana

Smoking marijuana produces similar effects to taking a hallucinogen. It increases heart rate. It distorts a person's sense of his or her surroundings. Marijuana also causes memory loss and can make a person feel paranoid (having an irrational mistrust of other people).

Over time, marijuana can damage a person's respiratory system, causing breathing problems and possibly cancer. It can also damage the immune system, which protects the body from disease and illness. Research also suggests that marijuana smokers are more likely to try other, stronger drugs, such as cocaine or heroin. It is referred to as a gateway drug, which means that it opens the door to the possibility of using more dangerous substances.

Narcotics

These drugs, including heroin, opium, methadone, and morphine, are painkillers. Like depressants, these drugs slow down the central nervous system. Some of the most potent drugs, narcotics have a heavy impact on the body and mind, which means that they are extremely addictive. At first, users feel euphoric, or happy, and drowsy. But other, dangerous effects follow, such as difficult breathing, convulsions, coma, and possible

Someone may use steroids to build bigger muscles, but the drugs make a user violent and moody.

death. The withdrawal symptoms are severe and include tremors, cramps, chills, and sweating. Narcotics are among the most addictive drugs because they are so strong and powerful.

Nicotine

Nicotine is found in cigarettes and chewing tobacco. These products are illegal to use for anyone under eighteen. Many people smoke cigarettes to relax, but in fact, nicotine increases heart rate and blood pressure. Like marijuana, cigarettes are considered to be gateway drugs. Studies show that more teens are starting to smoke at younger ages than ever before.

Smoking increases the risk of heart disease, emphysema, stroke, and cancer of the mouth, throat, lungs, uterus, and bladder. Cigarettes are extremely addictive and contain many harmful chemicals.

Steroids

Steroids are safely used to treat some diseases, such as anemia; however, they are often used illegally. Athletcs, in particular, use them illegally to heighten their performance, making their bodies bigger, stronger, and faster.

But steroids cause many health problems, such as liver tumors, jaundice (a yellowing of the skin), severe acne, and high blood pressure. Steroid users also experience periods of extreme paranoia, anger, and hallucinations. Long-term use can cause liver disease, cancer, and heart attack.

Stimulants

Stimulants include the drugs cocaine, crack, amphetamines, and prescription drugs like Benzedrine and Dexedrine. They increase the blood pressure and heart rate. Users feel alert and euphoric at first, but then suffer from hallucinations, convulsions, and possible death. Abusers become violent, anxious, and depressed, often losing interest in food and sex. Other dangerous effects include heart attack, stroke, and respiratory failure.

This is a brief look at some of the most commonly abused drugs. Teens start using drugs for many different reasons. Some like the high they feel from drugs. Others do it to fit in with a certain group of friends. Still others do drugs as a way to experiment or a way to rebel. Many believe drug use is a rite of passage—a natural and necessary part of experiencing life and becoming an adult. Even if your friends tell you how great drugs are, or if you decide it is harmless to try them a few times, you could get yourself into trouble. Using drugs can negatively affect all aspects of your life.

Chapter 2

Why Do People Use Drugs?

*J*ason and his friends liked to get together and play music. They wanted to start a band one day. Every weekend, they gathered in the basement at Jason's house to practice. One day, Danny, the guitarist, brought over some LSD he got from his brother. Before practice, everyone took a hit. Danny said it would help them play better and make the music more interesting. They were planning to write new songs that day.

About a half hour after he took the hit, Jason started to feel weird. He felt really restless, too. He had so much energy. He picked up his drumsticks, but he could not concentrate on the music. In fact, he didn't even feel like playing anymore. Everyone else was acting strange too. They all were jumpy, moving around the room. A few hours later, Jason began to feel sick. He started to sweat, then he threw up. Jason's friends were too "out

Many teens use a drug because they think it will make them more creative.

of it" to help him. Jason lay down for a while, but hours later he still felt awful. He had had no idea that the high lasted so long.

There are many reasons why some teens use drugs. This chapter looks at some of the most common ones.

Experimentation

When something is forbidden, most teens want to try it even more, especially if parents are the ones saying "Don't do that. It's bad for you." It's normal to want to experience new and different things. Everyone rebels against an authority figure at some time in their life. It's one way to find out who we are and create our own identity. When it comes to drugs, it can be very tempting to use them because those things promise to make you feel good.

Many teens believe they are expanding their horizons or increasing their creativity when they experiment with drugs. But the physical and chemical reactions that occur in the body and brain are often ignored or unknown by teens. They don't think about where the drugs go and what happens when they get there. To them, it's just a way to change their perceptions of reality. But it's important to be careful. Trying drugs just to see what they feel like can be very dangerous and lead to serious problems in your life.

Pop Culture Influences

Most likely you've heard about drugs. Television, radio,

and newspapers are filled with stories of movie stars, musicians, and athletes who use drugs. Popular movies such as *Trainspotting* and *Pulp Fiction* feature characters that use drugs. Movies often glamorize drug use and they have a strong influence on teens' view of drugs. Teens may underestimate the danger of drugs and mimic the actions that they see and hear. This is how some teens start taking drugs.

The most common drugs that teens first try are nicotine (cigarettes) and alcohol. Because these drugs are legal, many teens may not understand their harmful effects. Worse, some studies show that once a person tries one drug, he or she is usually willing to try other, more harmful drugs.

Dealing with Problems

If a person tries a drug and likes how it makes him or her feel, there's a good chance that the person will continue to use the drug. Being a teen isn't always easy. You may feel that your parents don't understand you, or that school is boring and a waste of time. You may be feeling depressed about your life or upset about a family problem. If you try a drug and it eases your pain or relieves your unhappiness, you may start using drugs regularly in an effort to cope with your situation. But in the end, the drug use will only make those problems worse.

Parents Who Drink or Use Drugs

Some teens grow up in homes where they often see their

Teens are surrounded by images that glamorize drug use.

It can be hard to resist the temptation to try drugs, especially when your peers are using them.

parents drink alcohol or use other drugs. Some parents may use alcohol responsibly, as many people do. But many others have problems with alcohol or drugs. Teens with substance-abusing parents may believe that drugs and alcohol are acceptable ways to cope with problems. They have learned this behavior from their parents.

Another risk factor is the fact that studies show that children of substance abusers are at higher risk than children whose parents don't have problems with drugs or alcohol. But, while these children are at higher risk for alcohol or drug-abuse problems, according to most studies today, genetic factors alone do not cause severe problems. Although scientists continue to conduct studies looking for specific genes that cause certain behaviors, they believe that abuse and addiction involve a combination of several factors. Still, children of substance abusers are not out of danger. Those who develop substance abuse problems of their own do so at an earlier age. Their problems tend to be more severe, as well.

Peer Pressure

The most common reason that people start using and continue to use drugs is influence from friends. You may find that a lot of what your friends do has an effect on you. If a teen is part of a group which values drug use, it can be pretty hard not to use drugs, and still feel accepted by people in that group.

Other teens may feel alone and left out of a group. Wanting to fit in or look cool to others, they start using drugs. It's hard to deal with peer pressure because it can be very subtle. In other words, many teens may not realize or recognize when they're succumbing to peer pressure. It can feel very natural to take a hit off a joint or have a beer when hanging out with friends. But soon these activities become a regular occurrence, and then you don't feel comfortable not using when you're with your friends. Your friends may make you feel unwelcome if you don't participate in their drug use.

Dealer Pressure

Many teens know of dealers in their school or on their street. Sometimes a dealer targets certain people and

offers them drugs free or for very little money. The dealer wants a person to become hooked, and then buy drugs
at a much higher cost. In this way, the dealer can make
a lot of money. Some dealers can be very convincing, and
teens find it difficult to resist the pressure.

The important thing to remember throughout this
book is that all the drugs described here are addictive.
You can easily become "hooked" on them, and once
you're hooked, it's hard to stop.

Chapter 3

Problems Caused by Drug Abuse

From what you've read so far, you know that any drug that changes how a person thinks and feels can be harmful. Drugs may cause physical, psychological, and legal problems. This chapter will look closely at those specific problems.

Physical Problems

The physical problems that drugs cause may be divided into three groups. These are loss of physical coordination, violence, and illness.

Loss of Physical Coordination

Physical coordination means your ability to control your movements. Some drugs have a harmful effect on this ability. For example, alcohol, marijuana, depressants, narcotics, and inhalants can slow your reaction time. These drugs also weaken your control over your muscles. Being high on any of these drugs can be very dangerous. It is not safe for you to drive a car, operate machinery, or be involved in any other activity that requires good coordination. Anyone high on these drugs increases the chances of having accidents of hurting him- or herself and others.

Violence

Certain drugs may cause people to become violent towards others. For example, cocaine, crack, and amphetamines cause people to become very angry easily. This often leads to violence. Steroids also cause people to be aggressive. A person taking these drugs easily gets into arguments and fights. This is often referred to as "roid rage." It's very scary because a person loses control over his or her emotions. Sometimes drugs even cause people to be violent toward themselves. When people come down from cocaine or amphetamines, they often go into a deep depression. They may attempt suicide.

Illness

Drugs damage your body and can cause many types of illness:

- Alcohol can cause cirrhosis and cancer of the liver.
- Cigarettes can cause ulcers, bronchitis, emphysema, heart disease, and many forms of cancer.

Some drugs will cause a user to become violent toward a friend or family member.

- Hallucinogens can cause heart and lung failure and convulsions.
- Inhalants can cause abdominal pain, brain damage, and hepatitis.
- Stimulants can cause heart attack, stroke, brain seizure, and respiratory failure.

Drugs also lower your immune system, which helps fight illness and disease. In addition, many drug abusers don't take care of themselves. To them, drugs are more important than food or sleep.

Inhibitions

Many drugs lower your inhibitions. Inhibitions are

Some teens may do things they wouldn't normally do while on drugs.

internal warning signals that help a person decide what he or she feels comfortable doing. Take those inhibitions away, and a person may be more likely to try other drugs, engage in criminal behavior, or have unprotected sex. A drug affects your ability to weigh the consequences of your actions. You may find yourself dealing with a jail sentence, an unwanted pregnancy, or a sexually transmitted disease.

AIDS (Acquired Immunodeficiency Syndrome)

In this age of HIV and AIDS, there is an extreme risk with some narcotics, such as heroin, of contracting the HIV virus. This is because heroin is often injected with a needle. Needles are commonly shared among heroin users and not properly cleaned. Small amounts of blood can be left on the needle, making it easy to transmit the disease, which is passed through blood and sexual fluids.

If you do drugs or have unprotected sex you will be at a very high risk of becoming infected. HIV and AIDS have spread at incredible rates. In 1996, 50 percent of all new infections occurred in young people between the ages of thirteen and twenty-four. And while there are promising treatments for AIDS, there is no cure.

Psychological Problems

Drugs affect how you think and feel. Drug abuse causes several types of mental and emotional problems, including loss of interest in things, memory problems, guilt and depression, anxiety and denial.

Drug abuse can cause many psychological problems, such as depression.

For example, drug abuse causes a loss of interest in school, sports, and other social activities. Drug abusers often show apathy. This means a loss of interest in everything—except drugs. Many abusers drop out of school or lose their jobs. You may know someone who went to school with you, got into drugs, and then dropped out.

Denial

Most drug abusers don't think they have a problem. They may feel bad, or guilty about their behavior, but they have no idea how to stop it. To cover up feelings of isolation and guilt, many abusers deny their problems.

Denial is a defense mechanism that many abusers use to continue their drug abuse. To admit their problems means that they have to do something about the problems. This is a very difficult realization for drug abusers to make. Instead of admitting their problems, they make up excuses and blame others for them.

Do I Have a Problem?

Here are some questions to ask yourself if you think you might have a problem with drugs and alcohol:

1. Do you use drugs on a regular basis?
2. Are drugs important to you?
3. Do you use drugs when you are alone?
4. Do you use drugs to help you relax or escape your problems?

5. Do you worry if you can't get drugs?

6. Do you mix drugs to get a stronger, more intense high?

7. Do you seek out parties and places where people are using drugs?

8. Have you lied to your family or friends to cover up your drug use?

9. Do you arrange your life around getting high?

10. Do you believe you can control your drug use?

11. Do you get high even when you promise yourself you won't?

12. Do you get angry when people say you have a drug problem?

If you've answered yes to more than three of these questions, there could be a serious problem. You should consider seeking help for drug abuse.

Legal Problems

Teens abusing drugs often don't care about anything else. Drugs cause them to become indifferent to their lives. Stealing and abusing drugs is against the law. If you are caught taking drugs or stealing money to buy them, you are risking your future.

Because of the rise in crime by young people, many courts are giving harsher punishments to juveniles. Even if you are under eighteen, you may face jail time for drug abuse. Having a criminal record can hurt your chances of being admitted to college or getting a job.

Here are a couple of questions to ask yourself: If you are a person who doesn't use drugs, are you thinking about using them? If you are thinking about using them, what are your reasons? What do you know about drugs? If you are already using drugs, are they causing problems in your life? What were the reasons you started using them in the first place?

If teens use drugs when they are alone, it is usually a warning sign for drug abuse.

Chapter 4

When Drug Abuse Becomes Drug Addiction

Many drug counselors and former drug addicts say that nobody makes a decision to become addicted to drugs or alcohol. It isn't a conscious decision. In other words, nobody plans to become addicted to drugs and alcohol. If you're abusing drugs, it can happen without your realizing it. The longer you use drugs, the more you need them. Soon drugs take control over your life, and you find you can't stop using.

Tolerance

If you continue taking drugs, your body soon develops a tolerance to them. Tolerance means that you need to use more and more of the drug to get the original effect. For example, at first, a couple of drinks may be all you need to feel good. But soon you find that you need much more than that to get the same feeling. Maybe you need to mix drugs to feel high. This is even more dangerous, because many abusers are unaware of the reactions their bodies may have to taking combinations of certain drugs. In this case, there is a higher risk of overdose.

Some abusers take other drugs to relieve withdrawal symptoms. For example, people addicted to heroin may take depressants to ease their discomfort when they come off heroin. A person's tolerance becomes higher and higher the longer he or she abuses drugs, which increases the threat of addiction.

What is Drug Addiction?

Drug addiction has two parts. One is psychological addiction, and the other is physical addiction. Both aspects make it very difficult to stop using drugs.

Psychological Addiction

Psychological addiction is needing to use a drug in order to feel normal. You need a drug to function and feel good. For example, you may feel that you cannot have fun at a party unless you're drunk or high. Or you may believe that the only way for you to mellow out is to smoke a joint.

If you cannot wait to use drugs, or if you think a lot about using, you are psychologically addicted. You want to be high or drunk as often as you can. You may show up at work or school under the influence of drugs. You may use drugs while you're at school or work. Drugs are always in the back of your mind. Much of your lifestyle revolves around using drugs or alcohol.

Physical Addiction

Physical addiction is when your body needs a drug in order to function. If you stop using the drug, your body goes into withdrawal. The body becomes accustomed to the drug, and the addict, without the drug, feels sick and experiences one or more of the following symptoms: nausea, sweating, confusion, depression, insomnia, chills, cramps, and disorientation. Withdrawal from depressants is especially dangerous. If abusers try to quit without the proper medical treatment, they risk death.

The Stages of Addiction

As a person becomes addicted to a drug, he or she goes through four stages. For some people, it takes several years to go through these stages. Others go through them in a few months. This is because it is easier to become addicted to some drugs than others. Crack and heroin are drugs that a person can become addicted to very easily, even after using them only one or two times.

Stage I

At first, you begin using a drug here and there, and mainly for fun. You basically do it because your friends do. You don't have any major problems because of your drug use. There are other things in your life like hobbies, sports, or school. Your drug use doesn't yet interfere with these activities. Some people always stay at this stage. Many teens go through a stage of experimenting with

Withdrawal symptoms are the major factor behind physical addiction.

drugs, and then they stop. Others, however, really like what drugs do for them. They end up using more and more. When this happens, they move into the second stage, which brings them closer to addiction.

Stage II

Now you find yourself needing more of the drug because your tolerance has increased. Small amounts are not good enough. It takes more to make you high or drunk. In order to increase the high, you begin using other drugs. For example, most drug users start with alcohol. Some use marijuana. In this second stage, it's not uncommon to try drugs like LSD, cocaine, or ecstasy. You find yourself thinking about drugs, even when you are not using.

Drugs start to interfere with school or work. You lose interest in school and you cut class. If you're working, you may be late, miss work, and eventually get fired from your job. You no longer hang out with friends who don't use or drink. You mainly want to be with using or drinking friends. A lot of your money goes toward buying drugs. Things that used to interest you no longer do. You also find yourself feeling more uptight and suspicious. You argue more with people, especially your family. Addiction is starting to set in.

Stage III

By now, drugs are more important than just about anything else. It takes large amounts to get high or drunk.

This costs money. You may start selling drugs as a way of getting money. You may do other illegal things to get money. Some drug abusers turn to prostitution to get drugs.

During this stage, most drug abusers have dropped out of school or lost their jobs. Many leave home or get kicked out. If you're still living at home, there is a lot of arguing. Drug withdrawal occurs. You feel a lot of depression and anger, and you're always uptight. The only way to make these feelings go away is to use more drugs. But the depression and anger always return.

Stage IV

Your drug use is completely out of control. Nothing else is important to you. Your body is so used to drugs that it is hard to get a high. Anger, suspicion, and depression are with you every day. Whenever you come down from drugs, the feelings are there.

Physically and mentally, you feel very run down. Thoughts of suicide come and go. You've had trouble with the law. Maybe you've even been arrested. It's hard to get money for drugs. You will do anything you have to to get drugs. When you run out of them, withdrawal is terrible. Some people make suicide attempts and end up in the hospital. Some people end up in jail. At this point, addiction must be treated with medical and psychological help. If it is not treated properly, addiction can result in death.

Can't I Just Stop Using?

It is easier to stop using drugs in the first stage, and harder in the second. Once you are in the third or fourth stage of addiction, it is very hard to stop.

When you are addicted to drugs, you are trapped in the drug cycle. You use a drug to get a high (to feel good). But problems often occur; arguments, fights, no money, quitting school, losing a job, depression, anger, guilt, etc. You use more drugs to get rid of these feelings. More problems occur, and so on. Some people feel trapped in their drug use. They feel hopeless. They believe there is no escape. If you are feeling trapped in your drug use, you may believe that no one can help you. But there is help. Many people find the help they need and recover. The next chapter will tell you what happens in recovery and how to stay away from drugs altogether.

Chapter 5

Quitting Drugs

Both drug abuse and drug addiction cause serious problems for people. But even though they have problems from their drug abuse, many people don't want to quit. For them, the good feelings caused by drugs are more important. They are willing to experience problems from drugs, because nothing outweighs the high. The drug is the most important thing in their lives. They continue to use and use, and get into more and more trouble. Many die from their drug abuse. They may overdose, commit suicide, or die from an illness or violence caused by drugs.

Other individuals enjoy the high feelings from drugs, but they don't want the problems. They try to cut back on their drug use. These people hope to avoid problems by using less. They try to use small amounts of a drug. They try to use drugs only when they think it is safe to do so. They say to themselves that they won't use drugs before or during school. They say that they will control how much they take. But it can be very difficult to control drug use. In the worst case, drugs take away any control you have over your life.

Some people are in Stage II of drug use. They abuse drugs, but they are not yet addicted. They may be successful in cutting back. You may promise yourself that you'll only use small amounts of a drug. You may say to yourself that you'll only use drugs at certain times. Or maybe you try a different drug and think you won't have a problem with it. This might work for a time. But soon, your drug use will sneak up on you. Gradually, you'll use more and more. Soon, you'll be using the same amount that you promised yourself you wouldn't use. Maybe you'll use more than ever before.

Why Do People Stop Using Drugs?

Many people stop using drugs. They come to realize that the high is not worth the problems caused by their drug abuse. They finally see that drugs cause more harm than they are worth. Some people have to hit rock bottom before they realize they have a problem. Maybe they are arrested. Or maybe they lose a job, or get kicked out of school. Maybe they end up at a hospital. Sometimes they lose a boyfriend or girlfriend because of their drug abuse.

If you abuse drugs, and there are people who care about you, they may hold an intervention. They and a counselor meet with you and force you into treatment. It is not because they are mean. It is not because they are trying to control you. It is because they care. Sometimes an intervention is done by a parent. Sometimes it is done by a teacher or a school principal. Sometimes the courts intervene and sentence you to drug treatment.

You may voluntarily try to quit using drugs, or you may be forced into quitting. Either way, it takes hard work and dedication to stay straight. Some people are able to stop using drugs on their own. They decide to quit, and they stick with it. Others need help. For these people, treatment programs are available. Some treatment programs are outpatient. This means that you visit the treatment program a few times a week for a few months. Other programs are inpatient. This means that you live in the treatment building while you receive treatment.

Treatment for Drug and Alcohol Abuse

People in treatment go through four stages. The first stage is coming off of drugs. Some people come off of drugs without too much trouble. However, others go into drug withdrawal. This often happens with people who have been using drugs for a long time. Drug withdrawal makes them feel sick. Different drugs produce different types of withdrawal symptoms.

For example, withdrawal from cocaine usually causes a person to feel depressed, nervous, and very uptight.

Friends can help a drug abuser realize there is a problem and urge him or her to get help.

Sometimes the person becomes suicidal. Withdrawal from narcotics causes people to sweat, feel sick to the stomach, and shake. Other drugs have other uncomfortable effects. Some drugs are easier to quit. Other drugs have withdrawal that can be severe enough to cause death. That is why treatment programs have doctors to help people come off of drugs safely.

Once drug withdrawal is over, the individual enters the second stage of treatment. It is here that the person is helped to really accept that he or she has a problem with drugs. Remember that most drug users are in denial. They like the high so much that they refuse to believe that drugs cause problems. Treatment helps people look at drugs for what they really are.

There are many groups that allow members to share their experiences and support each other as they quit drugs.

People use drugs because they like how drugs make them feel. They don't use drugs to have problems. But trouble does occur. This usually causes the drug abuser to feel guilty and depressed. To get rid of these feelings, the person uses even more. When people stop using drugs, they have to face and solve their problems. They also have to deal with all sorts of uncomfortable feelings caused by these problems.

The third stage of treatment helps people deal with these feelings. It also helps them sort out their problems and to find solutions. By now, the person in treatment is starting to feel a little better. But there is more to do. People who give up drugs, but don't make changes in how they live, usually start to use again. This is called a relapse.

During the last (fourth) stage of treatment, the person learns to make friends with people who don't use. He or she learns how to have a life without drugs.

Self-Help Groups

If you are committed to quitting and have taken the first steps to recovery, you can stay off drugs. It's important to remember, however, that an abuser also needs to enter a recovery program. Groups such as Alcoholics Anonymous and Narcotics Anonymous offer help. Their programs give patients tools to deal with recovery. Patients learn new types of behavior and receive support from others who have had similar experiences.

These twelve-step programs teach their members that drug and alcohol addiction are ongoing problems.

One of the best ways to stay away from drugs is to have drug-free friends.

There is no cure. Recovery is a continuing process that takes much work. These programs give members the support they need to stay drug-free. But the members must also come to terms with many things.

The Twelve-Step Philosophy

In a twelve-step program, members:

- admit that their lives have got out of control
- believe that they can change and get better
- agree to work with others to change their behavior
- make a list of destructive behaviors as well as positive qualities
- share the list with a trusted person
- decide to leave old behaviors and attitudes in the past
- work at changing old behaviors and attitudes
- recognize those who have been hurt by their behavior and apologize to them
- take responsibility for their problems and forgive themselves
- admit when they are wrong
- work on being a better person without drugs
- help others

Studies show that those who participate in self-help groups have a higher success rate at staying drug-free. Overall, the programs help people take control of their lives and give them the power to make positive changes.

Chapter 6

Staying Straight

It's not always easy to stay away from drugs. Sometimes the pressure to use can be pretty heavy. You have to make some tough choices in your life. In the process, though, you may learn how much you care about yourself and your future. You may find that respecting yourself means staying drug-free.

Why Is It So Hard?

If you use drugs, there's a pretty good chance that your friends also use drugs. Most of what you do with your friends probably involves drugs. When you stop using drugs, your friends may put pressure upon you to change your mind. They may not like your wanting to stay straight. They may not want to spend time with you unless you use with them. In other words, these so-called friends may not respect your desire to quit drugs.

Not having any non-using friends, you may feel very much alone.

Most major cities have support groups for teens who want to quit using drugs.These groups are made up of people who want to quit using and who feel very alone. By coming together, they support one another in staying straight, and friendships are often made. School counselors or teachers usually know how to get in touch with such groups.

Stress

Most regular drug users come to rely upon drugs to help them handle stress. If they are feeling uptight, or angry, or depressed, they use drugs to make the feelings go away. The uncomfortable feelings usually return, but there are always more drugs around to take.

If you use drugs regularly and you decide to stop, you will have to learn how to deal with stress.You may not be used to handling stress without drugs. Most people do not stop using drugs until they run into problems. Of course, problems cause you to feel stressed out.You'll have to face and solve these problems, and that can be pretty hard.

For example, let's say that a person has been high on drugs, and he has hurt people several times by lying or robbing those who trusted and loved him. He then makes the decision to quit drugs but feels guilty about how he has acted. He knows that he has to apologize to these people.That isn't easy to do. It forces a person to

Individual therapy is a very useful tool when a person is recovering from a drug addiction.

confront feelings that cause shame and embarrassment. But it's a necessary part of starting a new, drug-free life.

There are many people around who can help you. The Where to Go for Help section at the end of this book is a good place to start.

Overconfidence

Some people believe that quitting drugs is easy. They are confident that everything will be fine and don't seek out people to support them in staying straight. They may even continue to hang out with drug-abusing friends. Before they know it, they are back to using.

If you are using drugs, and you decide to quit, try not to be overconfident. Do not be afraid to ask others for help. This often makes the difference between staying straight and relapsing.

Even if you do not use drugs, you've probably run into them in one way or another. Because drugs are everywhere, it may seem like they are harmless. You may know some regular drug users who seem to be doing okay, but many regular drug users put on a front of having it together, but are really dealing with a lot of problems.

Whom Do You Hang Out With?

If you spend time with people who drink and use drugs, they'll most likely pressure you to do the same. They'll tell you that drugs are fun and won't cause you any harm. They'll be pretty convincing. However, if you hang out with people who do not use drugs, you can avoid being hassled. It may sometimes seem like most teens use drugs, but that is not true. If you really look around, you'll find that many kids in your school do not use. Having drug-free friends is your best defense against drug abuse.

You Don't Have to Defend Yourself

If someone is pressuring you to use drugs or to drink, and you don't want to, you don't have to spend time trying to defend yourself. Just be firm and keep it simple. You can say things like, "No thanks," or "I don't use," or "No way." Then just turn and walk away. Sometimes a person may bug you to use or drink, even after you

There are many other satisfying ways to spend your time that will enhance your life.

say no. This means that the person does not respect you and your wishes. Then you may have to be even more firm. Soon he or she will get the message.

Find Better Things to Do

If you're feeling bored and lonely, it's easy to slip into using drugs. But by filling your life with meaningful, fun activities, you may find you don't have time to waste on drugs. You may find that there are many different things to try that don't involve drugs, such as getting into art, music, dance, or a particular sport. Expressing yourself creatively will provide you with confidence and self-esteem.

Some people feel that the pressure to use is heavy. They don't know whether they can stay straight. If you find this is happening to you, your school counselor may be of help. Most counselors know of support groups for teens who want to stay free of drugs. If you do not use drugs, hopefully this book has taught you to remain drug-free. If you do use drugs, you can stop. The first step may be reading this book, the next one is to talk with someone whom you trust.

Glossary

addiction Dependence on a habit-forming substance so strong that its use causes physical and psychological problems.

asphyxia Loss of consciousness from lack of oxygen and excess of carbon dioxide in the blood.

central nervous system The part of the nervous system consisting of the brain and the spinal cord.

coma Deep unconsciousness from which a person cannot be roused; caused by disease or injury.

coordination Normal interaction of body parts, such as eyes and hands, for effective operation.

defense mechanism Mental process of the unconscious that enable a person to cope with painful problems.

denial Unconscious defense mechanism by which one refuses to admit painful thoughts, emotions, or facts.

disorientation Loss of ability to realize time, place, or one's own identity.

gene The unit of inheritance from parents of physical and mental traits.

hallucination Experience of unreal sights and sounds under the influence of certain drugs; delusions.

high State of elation or sense of power caused by use of a drug.

immune system Bodily system that protects the body from foreign invaders such as bacteria and viruses.

paranoia Mental disorder in which a person suspects others of having hostile intentions.

restriction Limitation of the right to use a substance or place.

stress Bodily or mental tension created by outside circumstances or events.

Where to Go for Help

Al-Anon/Alateen Family Groups
1600 Corporate Landing Parkway
Virginia Beach, VA 23454
(800) 356-9996
Web site: http://www.al-anon.alateen.org

Alcoholics Anonymous
P. O. Box 459
Grand Central Station
New York, NY 10163
(212) 870-3400
Web site: http://www.alcoholics-anonymous.org

American Council for Drug Education
164 West 74th Street
New York, NY 10023
(212) 595-5810 ext. 7860
(800) 488-DRUGS (3784)

Cocaine Anonymous
3740 Overland Avenue
Los Angeles, CA 90034
(310) 559-5833
Web site: http://www.ca.org

Narcotics Anonymous
World Service Office
19737 Nordhoff Place
Chatsworth, CA 91311
(818) 773-9999

National Association for Families
Addiction Research and Education
200 North Michigan Avenue
Suite 300
Chicago, IL 60601
(312) 541-1272

National Clearinghouse for Alcohol and Drug Information
P. O. Box 2345
Rockville, MD 20852
(800) 729-6686
Web site: http://www.health.org

Hot Line Numbers

The Cocaine Hot Line
(800) COCAINE (262-2463)

The National Institute on Drug Abuse
(800) 662-HELP

Teen Help
(800) 637-0701

Youth Crisis Hot Line
(800) 448-4663

In Canada:

Alcohol and Drug Dependence Information and Counseling Services (ADDICS)
#2, 2471 1/2 Portage Avenue
Winnipeg, MD R3J 0N6

Alliance for a Drug-Free Canada
#280, 55 Metcalfe Street
Ottawa, ON K1P 6K5

Council on Drug Abuse
698 Weston Road
Toronto, ON M6N 3R3

Narcotics Anonymous
P. O. Box 7500, Station A
Toronto, ON M5W 1P9

For Further Reading

Berger, Gilda. *Addiction*. New York: Franklin Watts, 1992.

Cohen, Susan and Daniel. *What You Can Believe About Drugs: An Honest and Unhysterical Guide for Teens*. New York: M. Evans, 1987.

Gilbert, Sara D. *Get Help: Solving the Problems in Your Life*. New York: Morrow Junior Books, 1989.

Grabish, Beatrice. *Drugs and Your Brain*. New York: The Rosen Publishing Group, 1997.

Harris, Jacqueline. L. *Drugs and Disease*. New York: Twenty-First Century Books, 1993

Rosenberg, Maxine, B. *On the Mend: Getting Away from Drugs*. New York: Bradbury Press, 1991.

Sexias, Judith. *Drugs: What They Are and What They Do*. New York: William Morrow and Co., 1991.

Challenging Reading:

Clayton, Lawrence. *Coping with a Drug-Abusing Parent*. New York: The Rosen Publishing Group, rev. ed., 1995.

Edwards, Gabrielle. *Coping with Drug Abuse*. New
    York: The Rosen Publishing Group, 1990.
Grosshandler, Janet. *Coping with Drinking and
    Driving*. New York: The Rosen Publishing Group,
    rev. ed., 1997
Kaplan, Leslie. *Coping with Peer Pressure*. New York:
    The Rosen Publishing Group, rev. ed., 1996.
Packard, Gwen. *Coping with Stress*. New York: The
    Rosen Publishing Group, 1997.

Index

About the Author

Dr. Herscovitch is a Clinical Psychologist who has been on staff with the Addictions Foundation of Manitoba in Winnipeg, Manitoba, Canada for twenty-two years. He also has a private practice and is an Assistant Professor of Psychology with the School of Medicine at the University of Manitoba. Dr. Herscovitch received his Ph.D. in Clinical Psychology from the University of Manitoba. He has lectured on the topics of alcoholism and chemical dependency in both Canada and the United States.

Photo Credits

Cover by Christine Innamorato; pgs. 2, 14, 28, 34, 52 by Ira Fox; pgs. 8, 21, 30 by Seth Dinnerman; p. 12 by Kathleen McClancy; pgs. 18, 54 by Ethan Zindler; p. 22 by John Novajosky; p. 27 by Sara Friedman; p. 38 by Megan Alderson; pgs. 46, 48 by Lauren Piperno.